Oohs, Ahhs, & Uh Ohs of Dating

Our Coffee House Conversations

Katherine White

&

Nakita Chante Wanza

Copyright © 2016 Sunny Smiles

All rights reserved.

ISBN-13: **978-0692530658**

DEDICATION

To everyone who has ever experienced the Oohs, Ahhs, and Uh Ohs of Dating. Our hope is that you identify with our stories and enjoy our Coffee House Conversations!

DEAR READER

We wrote the Oohs, Ahhs, & Uh Ohs of Dating Our Coffee House Conversations to share some of our experiences. This started out with two single entrepreneurs who met about business and apparently needed to chat about dating. The subject of dating became an unwritten topic on our agenda during each meeting. We laughed and we encouraged each other during those chats. After several moments of those Coffee House Conversations we started to think about other people who need to just have simple conversations about dating. Conversations without judgment and without pressure. Instead the conversations are positive and encouraging, of course, with a bit of humor…We encourage you to get with your colleagues, friends, and family to chat about your dating experiences. Keep those Coffee House Conversations going!

Katherine White and Nakita Chante Wanza

OOHS, AHHS, & UH OHS OF DATING OUR COFFEE HOUSE CONVERSATIONS

WHAT HAPPENS IN JAMAICA

SHOULD STAY IN JAMAICA 1

I'LL JUST CALL HIM GUMBO 4

HE HAD A FLIP PHONE 7

FRIENDLY EVER AFTER 9

LOVE RESISTS TEMPTATIONS 11

BE ME. NATURALLY 13

THE TAX GUY...OH MY 15

FRIENDS NOT LOVERS 17

WE CAN'T BE FRIENDS 19

MEET HIS MAMA 20

BUSINESS MAN 22

SWEETEST FRIEND ZONE 24

THESE LAST $2 26

JUST FRIENDS 28

THE ONE. STRIKE 1 30

THE ONE. STRIKE 2	32
RED FLAG	34
HE WAS FINE	37
EWW	39
THE RING	41
STACKS	44
HEART SHAPED BROWNIES	46
NAKITA CHANTE WANZA	49
KATHERINE WHITE	51

All quotes and lessons learned are originals written by us from our experiences in hopes of encouraging our readers…

Oohs, Ahhs, & Uh Ohs of Dating

WHAT HAPPENS IN JAMAICA SHOULD STAY IN JAMAICA

Oh Jamaica! What a beautiful place with beautiful people! One night, while vacationing there, I needed a band aid and alcohol to take care of a spider bite. That's another story. I approached one of the bar areas to ask for where those items could be found. A young man offered to walk me to the medic area and we chatted a bit. Finally we arrived and at that point I got a really good look at this man. Wow! He was fine. Really fine! I still wasn't paying attention for anything further until…He shook my hand after telling me his name and looked right into my eyes asking me to promise him we would see each other again. Whoa! He was fine, direct, and put me on the spot. So, of course I said yes with all smiles. Later we met on the beach near the snorkeling area. It was dark with a bit of light shining from the resort area. That totally felt like a scene from a romantic comedy but it was my life for a moment. We talked about our lives. Mine in the United States and his in the Caribbean. This guy showed me a picture of his adolescent daughter he took care of alone because her mother had passed away. I was sad for him and his daughter but admired how responsible he seemed to be. He also mentioned that he had a twin brother. This will be important later. I enjoyed the rest of my time on the beautiful island. This guy called me every day once I got back home. He was sweet but a bit much. He wanted to come to the states for better opportunities but I honestly did not care either way. I heard those stories and I was not hopeful or that invested. I did try finding him on social media and found a guy who looked just like him with a slightly different name. Let's just say his name was John and the profile names were Jonah. Very close but surely that could have been his twin right? Well, after further research I discovered pictures of the girl who was said to be John's daughter. The little girl he was taking care of alone since her mother was supposed to be dead. Right? I kept searching because this was kind of strange. Why was the little girl on Jonah's page so much but she was John's daughter? I started to look further. This little girl was connected to a woman's page who appeared to be her mother and very much so alive. Then I saw the woman who appeared to be the mother in a couple of photos with John not Jonah. So, when I talked to John I told him that I looked for him on social media and told him about my findings. This guy told me not to look at those pages because he and his brother share social media. REALLY? At that point I knew the guy apparently saw me as a fool and I realized he was insane. Who lies about the mother of their child being dead? I was like. Oh no. I cannot be involved with this guy at all. I ended it and never allowed further communication.

WHAT I LEARNED?

I never had expectations beyond Jamaica. I had a good time. I was aware of the infamous "island" dating games. I researched and found out the guy was a pathological liar and I cut ties immediately. I learned that some people should stay where they are.

"What happens in Jamaica should stay in Jamaica."

I'LL JUST CALL HIM GUMBO

I am going to cut to the chase with this guy. He was from New Orleans but I met him after he moved to Houston. He had a son who was about 1 years old at the time. I hadn't dated a man with children before but I was open that time. This guy epitomized deceit. He seemed to be financially stable, he had a very nice car, and he was kind of sweet. Like the "because I want something" kind of sweetness. I met this guy during a time where my schedule was too flexible. I needed something to do. Too much time on my hands resulted in us spending a ton of time together. That was a bad idea. A couple of things happened during this time of dating him. One day he called to tell me his car was stolen. I felt bad for him. I asked if he called the police and his insurance to file a claim. He did not but was already shopping for a new car. Red flag! So, I went to dealerships with him and everything. He didn't get another car and I later found out his car was repossessed. I never called him out because I thought maybe he was just embarrassed. Later, I figured he was just a liar. Then one of the two last things and the last straws for me was when I was doing some work on his laptop and went to open files that I saved. I came across his videos. This guy had like a gallery of videos of him and other women performing intimate acts. I was disgusted and thinking that I had no idea who this guy was. We talked about it and he assured me the videos were old but I was still very disturbed by his strange video collection. It wasn't respectful and I started to see him as some sort of a Hugh Heffner want to be. That isn't my type. The relationship was ending quickly. Last but not least. I was hanging out with him and he was sitting next to me responding to women on a dating site. I asked him about it and he denied it. So much that he should have just said my eyes were lying. I literally saw what he was doing. So, I left his place and never saw him again. He was filled with too many random ingredients and that's why I'll just call him Gumbo!

WHAT I LEARNED?

From the beginning this guy seemed to have just some of the qualities that I appreciate in a man. Just having some qualities should not be enough to get him through the door of a relationship. I learned to never settle for mediocrity.

"Mediocrity and greatness don't hang out."

HE HAD A FLIP PHONE

I would see this guy every time I would stop at a particular store on my way to work. He was handsome and sweet. One day he spoke to me at length. He asked about my perfume and complimented my smile. Cool. I was flattered. Then he asked for my number. I gave it to him because I mean he was cute and sweet. That's a start. I didn't judge him by his job. Because it could have been a part time job or something. I didn't know his situation. Then when I was giving him my number he pulled out his phone or should I say flipped out his phone to enter it. That's right! This guy had a flip phone. Now I wasn't trying to judge this guy by his phone either but it seemed to be getting worse as I discovered more about him. Moving forward. He called and we chatted a bit and I found out he had a little baby. Here we go. I wasn't very interested but I gave the guy a chance by getting to know him before deciding on moving forward. One day he called me to say he wished he had his car so that he could bring me lunch. I was like oh that's sweet but where is your car? He said he kind of had one but kind of did not. Of course I asked him to explain. He had a car but no motor and could not afford the motor or the car. In a nutshell. He did not have a car. This conversation was so juvenile to me. It was nostalgic and not in a good way. It made me think of my high school boyfriend wishing he could drive to see me. I was uninterested given the flip phone and all of the little things that had piled up.

WHAT I LEARNED?

I learned not to entertain someone who is interested just because they are interested.

"Interest and attraction are not enough for a relationship."

FRIENDLY EVER AFTER

I have found myself in the friend zone a couple of times. It's cool until it's not cool. So this one guy was super amazing. Everything checked out. Witty. Check. Smart. Check. Handsome. Career. Hilarious. Check. Check and check. He also seemed to be so into me until we had to have, "the conversation." You know the conversation is where you settle down with the light hearted fun talk or even political debates to discuss relationship goals. During the conversation. Very awkward might I add. He was clearly battling confusion, fear, or something. For a moment I was confused because he was but eventually I decided to make a decision since he was so freaking confused. I created boundaries and decided on total friend zone without benefits of course. We then lived happily and friendly ever after.

WHAT I LEARNED?

Decide on what you want or need and do not waiver because the other party is unsure of what they want or need.

"I want someone who may be afraid to love but is not afraid to try."

LOVE RESISTS TEMPTATIONS

Men are interesting in their expressions of love, feelings, and emotions. You know. The mushy stuff. My ex-boyfriend was very mushy if you will. Affectionate and would totally give me the shirt off his back if I needed it. We enjoyed each other's company and were supportive of each other but there was just one thing that kept getting in the way. How can I say this in the most politically correct way? He was a ladies man. He was addicted to the ladies. Yep and cheated often. He seemed to love me but the temptation of others was stronger than the love. That love was not love. Not true love anyway. I was always conflicted because we had the chemistry and we were good together but when he cheated I felt as though I wasn't good enough. Like I was falling short in areas. I would even compare myself to the women who I knew about to see what they had that I did not. Eventually, I finalized the relationship. It took time but I was freed from the insecurities and a constant broken heart.

WHAT I LEARNED?

I am good enough in all circumstances of relationships. One of the best pieces of advice that my Dad has given me about love is this. "A man's love for you keeps him there and it will make him resist temptations to be with someone else."

"Love will resist temptations for you."

BE ME. NATURALLY

I once went through a phase. "I was so heavenly minded that I was no earthly good." During that time I met an amazing and hardworking guy from the Caribbean. His accent was just oh my goodness good! He was handsome too. He expressed interest in me. We started to talk about hobbies and life. We always swapped healthy but yummy recipes. He cooked for too. Great guy! One day he asked me if I drink alcohol; like wine and rum (a Caribbean staple). I answered. I hit him with a good ole church girl, NO, to that question and a plethora of other pretty normal questions. The truth is that I said no because many of those things were associated with my past. I was so busy trying not to be like the old me that I was not being me. I had no balance between who I was and who I was becoming. It wasn't natural. He felt it. I felt it. In that process I met a good man who appreciated me but I was not nearly ready for him.

WHAT I LEARNED?

This was a hard lesson to learn. I had to make pride powerless and be honest with myself through self-reflection. I eventually learned to be me. Naturally. At every stage and in every phase.

"Authenticity trumps imitation."

THE TAX GUY…OH MY

I tried out a new tax preparer this one year. He was recommended by a friend so I was confident in his ability. Well, he and I connected on an intellectual level. He knew his stuff! I am attracted to a man's mind before anything else…as cliché as that sounds. We talked for hours about the economy, finances, and our personal aspirations. This guy really made an impression on me. We planned to meet at some of our places of inspiration like bookstores and coffee houses…go figure. All of this started with business. Well, to make a long story short. I was expecting a tax refund. Time kept passing and it was odd that I had not received it. Finally, I contacted the IRS after the tax guy and I mysteriously stopped chatting after my several attempts to contact him. The IRS representative informed me of the refund amount and disbursement date. She also mentioned the account of the disbursement and none of those numbers matched any of my accounts. This guy had stolen my money! Oh, I really contacted him then. He finally responded with lies about the processing fees and IRS fees. At that point he was insulting my intelligence especially because he was privy to my background and education from our intellectual conversations. He never refunded my funds. He did not apologize. I eventually just took it as a loss and moved on.

WHAT I LEARNED?

Be just as wise in dating as I am in business, especially, when the two are mingling. I learned how to forgive without an apology.

"Forgive even if they don't apologize."

FRIENDS NOT LOVERS

I met a young man after a step show during my first year in college. He was super tall, cute, and so cool. As time went on he and I spent so much time together. This guy totally appealed to my love language of quality time. We talked about everything. He was down to earth, cuddly, and my favorite trait of all…he was just a country boy going to school in the city. I loved his country charm and innocence. He had not been tainted by much. He just seemed like the perfect partner for a southern belle like me. We remained friends after college but he moved away. Whenever he was in my city we would meet and pick up conversations where we left off. Once, while he still lived in another city he contacted me about moving back to my city. He wanted us to give a relationship an official chance. That was tough because at one point in my life he had the key to my heart but I loved him enough to tell him no. Years later he married a beautiful lady. I had the "what if" thoughts for a bit but then I saw the purpose. We never crossed lines involving sex or physical intimacy in the past. He and I were meant to be friends not lovers. Platonic and supportive.

WHAT I LEARNED?

To be wise in love. Don't be so quick to be physically intimate. Cultivate and value the purpose of a friendship.

"I would rather lose a potential partner to keep an amazing friend."

WE CAN'T BE FRIENDS

My ex and I continued friendship after many break ups to make ups. We would hang out, have dinner, buy gifts, and even spend time together during the holidays. The only time we were not so close was when either of us were involved in relationships. That was out of respect and we were occupied. One day I had an epiphany and I finally decided to break up with my ex. I realized we could not be friends. Not because we had a fight or because I hated him. I actually loved him. We couldn't be friends because the strength of that love would not allow us to fully move forward. The decision to break up with my ex was just as emotional as our break up as a couple. However, I gained freedom from our relationship and our past that was being held together by that friendship.

WHAT I LEARNED?

Sometimes you can't be friends with your ex and truly move on.

"Freedom can be found in love from a distance."

MEET HIS MAMA

I met this guy in my first year of college just randomly on the yard. He wasn't my type or who I would usually be attracted to but he made me laugh and said he just wanted to talk. We went to his car to talk. Every time I said something about my life or goals he kept interrupting me with an ooh, or wow, or whaaat very loudly in that enclosed car! He was obviously impressed. I was flattered but the sound effects were a bit extreme for my taste. So after all of the dramatic oohs, whaaats, and wows he asked to take me out to eat. He said he would have to take a lady like me somewhere special. The restaurant he mentioned actually wasn't all that special but the thought was nice. He told me that before we would go to eat he wanted to take me to his mama's house so she could meet me. His mama! I had just met this man. He said he wanted to introduce us because of how much he liked me. The guy was coming on way too strong. I kindly and quickly refused the food at his special place as well as the mama introduction.

WHAT I LEARNED?

Just don't waste time.

"Don't become trapped by flattery."

BUSINESS MAN

I was doing business with this guy for some time but had not connected for a while. Well, we reconnected on business but started to connect on a spiritual level. Or so I thought. We attended church events together, prayed, and had deep conversations about purpose. More than business but less than personal. The development of this relationship was interesting. He was always impressed with my expertise and how I conducted business. We even talked under the stars and just started to hang out a great deal. He had just broken up with his girlfriend but lived with her. That kept me distant knowing there wasn't a chance that I would move forward beyond the friend/business thing. I was not with that. I drew the line when we were engaged in business dealings and he crossed the lines by trying to kiss me. He said he needed someone to hold him. So, I went back and hit him with all of that spiritual God stuff we had been discussing. I asked him questions like…Do you think this is really what God wants for you? Is this a part of our purpose for working together? That shocked him. It wasn't long before I ended the friendship with the business man.

WHAT I LEARNED?

Create boundaries and do everything within business hours.

"Boundaries lead to clarity and eliminates any confusion."

SWEETEST FRIEND ZONE

Oh my colleague turned friend and I were like two peas in a pod. He was so sweet to me. We went to lunch together, worked out, and swapped healthy recipes. It was friendly for so long and during most of the time he was in a relationship. That did not matter because we were totally just friends. Well, when his relationship ended he and I started to hang out more as well as talk more outside of working hours. I invited him to family functions and he would show up just as my friend. We would go out just one on one. He always told me that I was beautiful and deserved so many amazing things. He encouraged me through my dreams and goals. I always told him how great he was and encouraged him in his career. I was a positive voice of reason through his family issues and concerns. We were just there for each other. His sweet and kindness started to appeal to me. It made me wonder if he and I should try something further. Life was starting to change. Time was moving forward. Neither of us worked at the same firm anymore. He was eventually connected in a relationship. We truly had the sweetest friend zone.

WHAT I LEARNED?

He strongly appealed to my love languages but through that I learned not to take someone out of the friend zone just because they are sweet and appeal to my love languages.

"The friend zone was created to save friendships and avoid break ups."

THESE LAST $2

I was intrigued when I met $2. His conversation was refreshing, open, and honest. He was tall dark, and handsome with a nice body. This man was also intelligent, well-educated, and had an overall great spirit. We met while I was in search of a trainer who could help me get my body in shape for my big birthday. I was not looking to date but I am always open. He met me at a local restaurant and we talked for hours…Let me cut to the chase and explain why his name is $2. After a couple of days of training he asked me out to dinner and I accepted. I already had a feeling he wanted to have a serious conversation. So we met for dinner. After leaving the restaurant we walked around the area, picked up dessert, and that's when the deep conversation happened. We both agreed it was so refreshing to meet someone who could hold a conversation and talk about multiple topics. But, don't get too excited… The next couple of months were a whirlwind of workouts, dates, compliments, and admiration. We had dinners, went to movies, and attended a concert together. We were getting to know each other well. I thought we connected spiritually, mentally, and emotionally. Then I started to notice his emotions ranged from happy to downright depressing. I had to constantly motivate him, give him ideas, feed him, and wash his clothes. I know that was too much but at first I did not mind doing those things because I am a nurturer by nature. Then the last straw was when he asked for $20 to get some gas. Hell, I had just gotten laid off and he knew that but it did not stop him for asking me and countless others for money. I came to the conclusion that he was a user and a con artist. He specialized in getting over on people with kind and giving hearts. I am kind and a nurturer but I am not a fool. I left him alone with his last $2 and immediately ended what we had started.

WHAT I LEARNED?

Don't get caught up in what it sounds like. Get caught up in what it feels like.

JUST FRIENDS

I think every woman has a male friend she isn't attracted to beyond friendship. You enjoy his company but get uncomfortable when he tries to make a move or God forbid bring up the possibility of dating. Well, I had a friend I had known practically my whole life. We would have a blast growing up together then later in college. We went to parties, cracked jokes, and just hung with each other as friends. I had no idea this guy liked me for more than that until he told me. I straight up told him, NO, when he approached me with the dating conversation. As his friend I urged him to focus on his growing business. I mean as his friend but also to get his attention away from me related to the possibility of dating. He agreed, reluctantly, but it did not stop his pursuit at first. Then I went on multiple dates with him. Wrong idea! In my mind he was just a friend but in his mind he was getting closer to being more than that. Eventually, I had a detailed conversation with him. I told him how much I appreciated our friendship and going further would be risking our life-long friendship. He finally understood, moved on, and he is happily involved in a beautiful relationship.

WHAT I LEARNED?

To be honest, specific, and clear on what I want in relationships to avoid ruining valuable friendships.

THE ONE. STRIKE 1

I remembered in school he was a shy guy but handsome and a little mysterious. I would see him in passing but never really spoke until we connected after seeing his face on a social media site. I sent him a message and he responded. Within a couple of days he invited me to lunch. As I approached the restaurant I was hoping he remembered me and he did. We sat for lunch. The conversation was good and flowing but it's what transpired during lunch that had me thinking he could be the one! A couple sitting near us kept smiling and staring at us as we had lunch. After about 30 minutes of staring the woman came over and said there was a light around us. That was the sweetest thing and I was taken back. So was he. We all began to talk with each other like we had known each other for years. The mother, who was in her late 80's, started telling us about how to have a godly relationship and about her marriage of over 40 years. The conversation on how to have a Godly and long lasting marriage was humbling and enlightening. Because of that he and I started dating immediately thinking we had really found the "one" in each other. A week went by and we had several dates scheduled including a jazz concert that I was looking forward to. Not to mention it was Valentine's Day weekend. I hadn't had date for Valentine's in years and was excited. In the middle of the week he asked me to dinner. He had been traveling and wanted to see me. We decided on the location. Once we met he did not have a good attitude. Traffic on his way to the restaurant annoyed him then he ask my opinion about something and I told him the truth. He did not appreciate that which further contributed to his sour attitude. Turns out he didn't really want my opinion. He wanted my agreement. Oh boy did that cause a great divide. His lips were poked out and his arms were folded like a little boy. I had to keep asking him if he was alright. He said he was fine but I felt so uncomfortable and we ended the night early.

WHAT I LEARNED?

I learned to pay attention to his temperament. A man who pokes his lips out in conflict is not my ideal mate but the lessons continued with this one in strike 2.

THE ONE. STRIKE 2

Remember the weekend of activities planned? So, it was Friday and I met him 30 miles outside of the city. Naturally I thought the next day, Valentine's Day, he would pick me up. Uh...NO!!! He asked me to meet him because he was running late. I agreed to meet him. I was thinking maybe he was picking up a gift for me. Uh...NO...again!!! I arrived to no gift or acknowledgement of the day. I was pissed and we still had the jazz concert the next day. Because of this I didn't want to go but I loved the musicians playing plus he had already bought the tickets. I was still pissed and it kept piling on but the concert was amazing. He was resistant, did not want to dance, or express interest but I enjoyed the show. The entire time he sat there like a statue. Some days went by before he called and we decided to meet for dessert one afternoon. Before I could sit down comfortably he went in on how he planned the 3 day disaster of a weekend and I wasn't appreciative. Again, I was pissed. It was as if he rehearsed this before meeting to make sure he got his points across. We had already discussed it and were over that. I sat through his rehearsed speech of apparent built up anger. Once he finished I allowed him to walk me to my car and I knew I would never ever talk to that fool again. It turns out…He was not the one.

WHAT I LEARNED?

I learned that a man's temperament in conflict reveals who he is. I realized that I would not change him or continue trying to work something out with someone who holds grudges.

"I'm never disappointed when things don't work out. I just thank God and keep it moving."

RED FLAG

He was tall, handsome, educated, Cali born, and a member of my favorite fraternity. We met at his fraternity national convention in my hometown. He spotted my booty on the dance floor as he would tell me later. He was cute and could dance and I love a confident man with swag!!! He came behind me on the dance floor and asked me to dance. I agreed. We danced for hours, exchanged numbers, and planned to connect the next day. He called as planned and asked if I would stop by his hotel where I had met him the night before at the convention. I was already in the area and stopped by. He gave me a big hug. The we got onto the elevator and went to the top floor to take in the magnificent roof top view. Our conversation was good but he kept asking me to go to the pool which I thought was weird and a red flag but I excused it because he was a cutie. After that we talked at least every other day. He went back to Cali and I visited him. I love California! We had a great time doing all of the signature Cali things. During all of this I noticed he wanted me to be more touchy feely and I had just met him. Another red flag. I am affectionate but I have to gain some trust before I love all over you. I went back home and we continued our phone calls. We were dating from a distance. I traveled back to see him for my birthday. He picked me up from the airport and boy was he in tour guide mode. He planned everything from checking out the fashion district to wine tasting and dinner. More red flags were being thrown all over the place. Like when I accompanied him to work. He wanted me close to him at all times. He did not really want anyone speaking to me. On top of that he told me that my clothes were too bright. Really? The last straw was that he wanted me to grow my hair out. Hold Up! I had to let him know that I like bright clothes because I am not depressed. Furthermore, when he met me my hair was short and I had just cut it. To top it off he was not always dressed to impress. He wore shorts everywhere and all of the time. Who does that? The killer red flag on the play was his baby mama drama. Cali was nice and he was cutie but I was done after red flag after red flag.

WHAT I LEARNED?

Red flags are raised for a reason. I learned to pay attention even through the fun, the gifts, and the trips.

"Love is acceptance of yourself and all of your flaws."

HE WAS FINE

Have you ever met someone who was so fine you could just stare at them all day? This dude could have been on a billboard modeling jeans, underwear, or something. Yes. That kind of fine! On top of that he rode a motorcycle! I was really into dating and enjoying myself at that time, especially, since I was just ending a tumultuous relationship. He was the breath of fresh air that I needed. We didn't even see each other or talk much but I found myself more excited about his fineness than him…He wasn't the cutest and he didn't stimulate me mentally but I didn't care at that time. We would always run into each other at parties and on a couple of occasions he invited me to biker rallies which I enjoyed. Then one night, it happened, he invited me to come back to his place. I was too excited because all of our time up to that point was spent in groups. We got to his place and I immediately went to shower because we live in the south and the humidity is ridiculous. Plus, I wanted to be so fresh and so clean in case something went down. After getting fresh. I waited for him to finish up in the shower then we were finally ready for bed. He told me that he only slept naked. I was like oh okay. That's cool!

I was okay with that because the man was fine but nothing happened. At all! Not even a kiss. Nothing! Strange I know. The next morning I woke up, got my stuff, and couldn't wait to get into my car so I could tell my friend about what didn't happen. We were both in disbelief since he was so fine and we had mutual attraction. I came to the conclusion he must have been delusional. Honestly, I know that I was being protected from something. About a year later I heard from him and the feelings weren't the same. I had moved on but for sure had an unforgettable memory.

WHAT I LEARNED?

A fine man only goes so far. He has to have some substance. I learned that I was protected from something in that situation and I am truly grateful.

"God is loving and covering me."

EWW

My trusted friend, more like a sister, connected me with a guy for a blind date. Her God Father suggested him and since I trust them both I agreed to go along with this blind date. The gentleman eventually contacted me and we talked for a bit. Of course, I checked out his social media profiles and he really wasn't my type, however, my type wasn't getting me anywhere so I went with it. He invited me to a basketball playoff game. I eagerly accepted because I love going to cheer for the home team. He did inform me he was traveling but would be back in plenty of time for the date. On the day of the date, around 4:00pm, I hadn't heard from him. I didn't know if we were meeting for dinner, if he was picking me up, or if we would meet at the venue. Oh I was annoyed. Finally, around 5:00pm he called to inform me that he had purchased the tickets and he was almost home from traveling. I was thinking he was cutting it close but fine. He also said we couldn't meet for dinner because it was too late. He then asked if I could meet him at his home. I hesitated because I never like to go to anyone's home on the first, second, or third date. Reluctantly, I agreed. I made it there by 6:45pm which was the time we agreed upon and guess what? He wasn't ready! I drove into his apartment complex and had to call him because he forgot to give me his apartment number. I found it and parked. Then he called me to go inside because he was in the bathroom! Eww, I was like uh, no, I'll wait. I don't know if he was going number two, brushing his teeth, or getting out of the shower but that was too much. I waited another 15 minutes. By that time I was pissed! Who invites someone on a date and isn't prepared? A first date at that. He finally strolled out with a button down shirt, jeans, and church shoes...I waited all of that time for that man to walk out in church shoes. We were going to a basketball game and sneakers would have been so appropriate. Anyway, we went to the game and I enjoyed myself because it was a good game but when we pulled up in his driveway I thanked him then jumped out like Jordan!

WHAT I LEARNED?

Well, I learned that I have jump man skills like Jordan when it comes to a date gone wrong. I also learned not to settle. This guy was not what I wanted to begin with and he displayed qualities that were just not for me.

THE RING

I met him while waiting for my sorority sisters to celebrate our annual Christmas brunch. While I waited I saw him standing at the hostess stand preparing to be seated. He was tall, dark, and handsome. His camel cashmere coat is what really caught my eye. I love a confident man with style! As my friends were arriving he and I made eye contact. He tipped his hat and smiled. I didn't share the contact with my friends at the time because that was our time and I didn't want any interference. We finally got seated and the fun began. The handsome camel coat wearing man approached me and complimented my smile. Strangely enough he was wearing a ring on his ring finger. I quickly spotted it when he shook my hand. I quickly asked him if he was married. He told me no and explained that he was wearing a purpose ring. A what? All of us gasped because we had never heard of that before. After our shock and awe he gave me his card. I accepted and waited a couple of days before I contacted him because I was still new to the purpose ring thing. We agreed to meet the following Sunday at the same restaurant since we both enjoyed brunch. Brunch went very well. We kept in contact all week and planned to meet again on that following Thursday to catch a movie, however, plans changed when I got off work earlier than planned on Wednesday. So we changed the day and he asked me to go to his home because my job was not far. I agreed. His invite was an hour before I arrived so I assumed he would be ready. I was wrong! He met me in the parking lot, we walked up three flights of stairs, he opened the door, and stuff was everywhere. Laundry was all over the couch, stuff was on the floor, dining room table, and in the kitchen. Don't get me started on the bathroom. It was like a tornado had just been through there. I could tell he wasn't prepared and he was tired. So was I after working and driving through traffic. He finally got it together and asked me to leave my car so that we could ride together. I disagreed for a couple of reasons. Needless to say, I drove my car. We decided to go to a new movie theatre but he had to make a stop first. That was a long and frustrating ride for us both. Finally we made it to the theatre and the movie was sold out. By that time I was so annoyed and hungry. So we did the next best thing and decided on dinner. He bullied me into riding with him. I did so, not because he bullied me, but because the restaurant was just 5 miles from where we were. Or so I thought. Instead he drove to the same restaurant but the furthest location. I did ask him why in the world we were driving so far. The man told me I would see that it wasn't too far. Control freak was written all over this guy and he was getting on my last nerve. He was in fact much older than I initially thought. His mannerisms and lack of energy told it all. To make a long story short…a camel coat and tall physique was not enough to keep my attention.

WHAT I LEARNED?

I learned that I don't want to waste time. Mine or theirs.

STACKS

I met this fine chocolate specimen of a man. He had long dreads and the prettiest pearly whites I had ever seen. He was tall and built like a Greek god. We met at a local hang out and I was immediately interested. However, he was somewhat distant, I learned later he had a girlfriend at the time and didn't want to start anything until he closed that door. I commended him on that. Time went on and he was no longer in a relationship. We planned to hang out. He lived with his mother in a 2 bedroom apartment. Nothing was wrong with that while he worked to get on his feet but this guy had stacks. Not money stacks but he had the furniture from his previous apartment stacked in his one bedroom. This guy was too cheap to rent a storage unit. I remember asking him if it was safe. His couch and table could have easily fallen on his head while he was asleep. I mean come on. That was straight up crazy and had to be some sort of code violation! Our little romance didn't last long. Those stacks were too dangerous! I can't remember how it ended but I do remember seeing him, years later, working the door at a sporting event. Enough said.

WHAT I LEARNED?

I know what chemistry feels like and that was not it.

HEART SHAPED BROWNIES

He was tall, dark, handsome, educated, and successful. He didn't have kids and we had an instant connection. My dear friend introduced us because she knew my type. The handsome guy lived in another state but that wasn't a problem for me since I had family there and would be visiting them soon. So, my friend arranged a double date while I was there and we all met for dinner. When he walked in I was immediately attracted to him. He had a warm spirit, beautiful eyes with long lashes, and a quiet confidence. You could not tell me he was not the one. We all talked briefly and ate dinner. He and I exchanged numbers. I had an early flight the next day so I couldn't stay long but I was confident I would hear from him. When I returned home I texted him and so it begin. We started talking daily and connecting mentally, spiritually, as well as emotionally. We had so many things in common and I truly felt I had known him my whole life. He felt the same way. After a few weeks he decided he needed a vacation and wanted to spend time with me. I obliged and could not wait! He greeted me with the best tasting heart shaped brownies that he baked just for me. I was falling head over heels...When he arrived I felt so genuinely happy. The first night we had dinner and talked to each other for hours. We were mesmerized with each other. He was only with me for two days and our connection was so strong that I never wanted him to leave. Unfortunately, it had to come to an end...He was just out of a relationship and because of everything he was dealing with we could not continue. That brief, yet, unforgettable relationship taught me how I should always be treated and I hope it taught him too.

WHAT I LEARNED?

He was in my life briefly just to show me what I deserve. As beautiful as that was; he wasn't meant to stay.

"If they were meant to stay they never would have walked away."

Our Coffee House Conversations

NAKITA CHANTE WANZA

Reflection...

I was sitting in my office trying to recall the last time I was in love. I mean truly in love. In love with an entire being. His good, bad, and ugly. Then I started to wonder how I measured love, especially, since I never really had a sense of what unconditional love was from my father. Had I really been in love? Or did I just romanticize about the thought of love? I find it refreshing to ask myself why I am the way I am in relationships.

Process...

I have done an in-depth inventory of my heart and mind. I have started to strip away the layers of heartache, disappointment, abandonment, rejection, and the hope of what could have been. When I looked back on past relationships, I do recall some great loves of my life but I remember wanting to be wanted and needed. Plus, I wanted to be in the exclusive group because I thought there was a certain level of respect if I were to be married like them.

Now...

Now, I am not interested in being wanted, needed, or being accepted into some exclusive group. I don't want to be like them. Who are they anyway? I am interested in a healthy, loving, supportive, and encouraging relationship that moves rhythmically as if we move to the rhythm of our own song. I don't want to try and make it work. It just does.

KATHERINE WHITE

Reflection...

I was approached by a man who was not my type or in my age bracket. I am talking like my parent's age. I entertained the thought of just going out with him but it was in a very nonchalant kind of way and not nearly like something I would do. A day or so later I found out disturbing news about his background and instantly I started to question everything about my dating life. Why did I attract who I attracted? Why did I give so and so a chance? Or why did I give the other guy so many chances and so much of my time? It was like an emotional wake up call. That nonchalant dating moment revealed a disturbance that ultimately jolted me into dating maturity.

Process...

I often take time to think about my life. I think about where I am and where I would like to be. Who I am and who I am becoming. The profound stuff. I had not done a seriously good job at this introspection when it came to the subject of dating. Then a couple of things had to happen for my dating maturity. I discovered how self-love impacted my life and how I viewed or conducted myself in dating. So, I worked on that part of my life. I realized my worth and walked in it. Then I decided that I no longer wanted mediocrity in dating and it had less to do with anyone else. This was all about love for myself, what I desired, and being true to my purpose. I considered that just casually dating someone who did not fit into my circle of purpose could easily become a casualty of love. As I have grown in my life, career, and business. I also had to grow up and prepare to be successful in relationships.

Now...

Dating, like life, is a journey. I am still learning. What I know for sure is that my connections must have life-giving purpose. I look forward to experiencing reciprocity and longevity in love.

ONLY THE BEGINNING…

www.ingramcontent.com/pod-product-compliance
Lightning Source LLC
LaVergne TN
LVHW051202080426
835508LV00021B/2770